SandCastle

Keeping the Peace

Dealing with Bullies

Pam Scheunemann

Consulting Editor, Diane Craig, M.A./Reading Specialist

ABDO
Publishing Company

Published by ABDO Publishing Company, 4940 Viking Drive, Edina, Minnesota 55435.

Printed in the United States.

Credits
Edited by: Pam Price
Curriculum Coordinator: Nancy Tuminelly
Cover and Interior Design and Production: Mighty Media
Photo Credits: BananaStock Ltd., ImageState, Stockbyte

Library of Congress Cataloging-in-Publication Data

Scheunemann, Pam, 1955-
    Dealing with bullies / Pam Scheunemann.
        p. cm. -- (Keeping the peace)
    Includes index.
    Summary: Describes different ways that bullies hurt others, physically or emotionally, and how to deal with these actions.
    ISBN 1-59197-560-3
    1. Bullying--Juvenile literature. 2. Conduct of life--Juvenile literature. 3. Peace--Juvenile literature. [1. Bullying. 2. Conduct of life. 3. Peace.] I. Title.
BF637.B85S37 2004
303.6'*--dc22
                                                                    2003057786

SandCastle™ books are created by a professional team of educators, reading specialists, and content developers around five essential components that include phonemic awareness, phonics, vocabulary, text comprehension, and fluency. All books are written, reviewed, and leveled for guided reading, early intervention reading, and Accelerated Reader® programs and designed for use in shared, guided, and independent reading and writing activities to support a balanced approach to literacy instruction.

Let Us Know

After reading the book, SandCastle would like you to tell us your stories about reading. What is your favorite page? Was there something hard that you needed help with? Share the ups and downs of learning to read. We want to hear from you! To get posted on the ABDO Publishing Company Web site, send us e-mail at:

sandcastle@abdopub.com

SandCastle Level: Transitional

Treating others
as you would like
others to treat
you keeps the
peace.

A bully teases or picks on other people.

Bullies can be girls or boys.

Bullies try to upset others.

Eric stays away from kids who are bullies.

Bullies spread stories about others.

Molly feels bad that Trish and Lynn are talking about her.

Bullies usually pick on one person, not groups of kids.

Molly finds some new friends to play with at recess.

Bullies don't let others play in their games.

Roger feels left out when some boys will not let him play ball.

Other kids on the team
know it is good to
include everyone.

Roger is happy he
can join the baseball
game.

Sometimes bullies try to hurt others.

Bob and Matt hit Ted on the playground.

If a bully hurts you, tell a grownup about it.

Mike talks to his dad about a bully at school.

Diane doesn't let bullies bother her.

She stands up for herself.

What can you do to keep the peace?

Glossary

game. an activity with rules that can be played by one or more people

include. to take in as part of a group

spread. to make widely known

tease. to annoy or make fun of another person

upset. to cause another person to be bothered or worried

About SandCastle™

A professional team of educators, reading specialists, and content developers created the SandCastle™ series to support young readers as they develop reading skills and strategies and increase their general knowledge. The SandCastle™ series has four levels that correspond to early literacy development in young children. The levels are provided to help teachers and parents select the appropriate books for young readers.

Emerging Readers
(no flags)

Beginning Readers
(1 flag)

Transitional Readers
(2 flags)

Fluent Readers
(3 flags)

These levels are meant only as a guide. All levels are subject to change.

ABDO
Publishing Company

To see a complete list of SandCastle™ books and other nonfiction titles from ABDO Publishing Company, visit **www.abdopub.com** or contact us at:

4940 Viking Drive, Edina, Minnesota 55435 • 1-800-800-1312 • fax: 1-952-831-1632